Neko and the Twiggets

By Donna Hoke

Illustrated by Jessica Gadra

All Rights Reserved

Text © 2010 by Donna Hoke

Artwork © 2010 by Jessica Gadra

No part of this volume may be reproduced or transmitted in any form or by any means, graphic, electronic, or mechanical, including photocopying, recording, taping, scanning, or by any information storage retrieval system, electronic or otherwise, without the written permission of the author and the artist, who own all rights to their individual contributions, whether verbal or graphic.

Printed and bound in Canada

ISBN 978-0-9839914-0-3 (Hard cover)

ISBN 978-0-9839914-1-0 (Soft Cover)

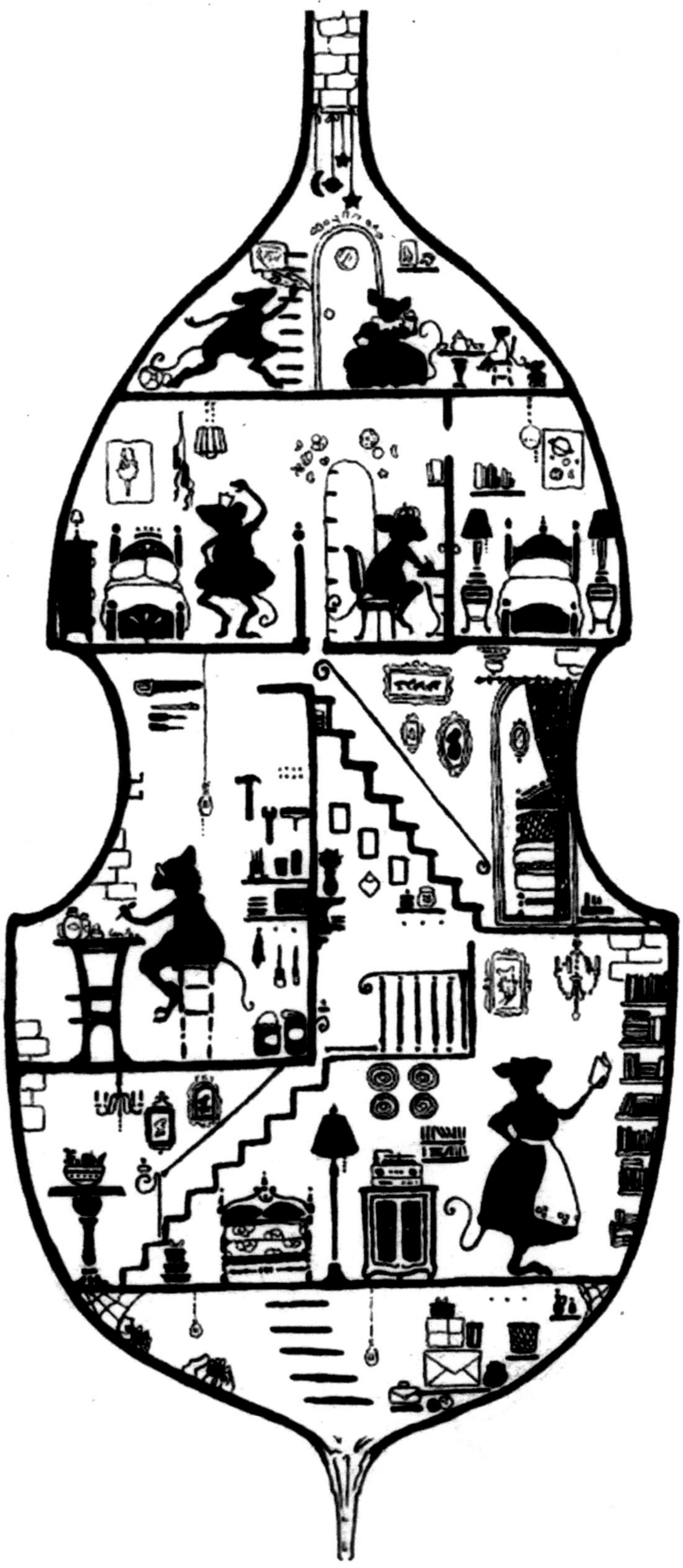

To the real Neko and all of my twins.

Dear Parents:

Thank you for choosing *Neko and the Twiggets* to read with your child. I hope that it encourages you to explore and discuss music in ways that you haven't before. Initial conversations about the instruments that comprise an orchestra, their sizes, and how they work can naturally lead to discussions about the music itself.

I have chosen to include the specific names of both composers and their works in *Neko and the Twiggets*. Even if the names are unfamiliar, their early introduction will increase recognition—and perhaps curiosity—as your child grows. Ideally, I hope that you and your children will find the pieces online (check YouTube), listen to them together, and discuss the images they evoke as well as the storytelling nature of classical music.

Finally, I hope that children will recognize, as Neko ultimately does, the importance of music in one's life—in any capacity. Whether or not your child chooses to play an instrument, he or she can still learn to appreciate the beauty that sound can create in nature, on stage, anywhere.

Thank you for reading,
Donna Hoke

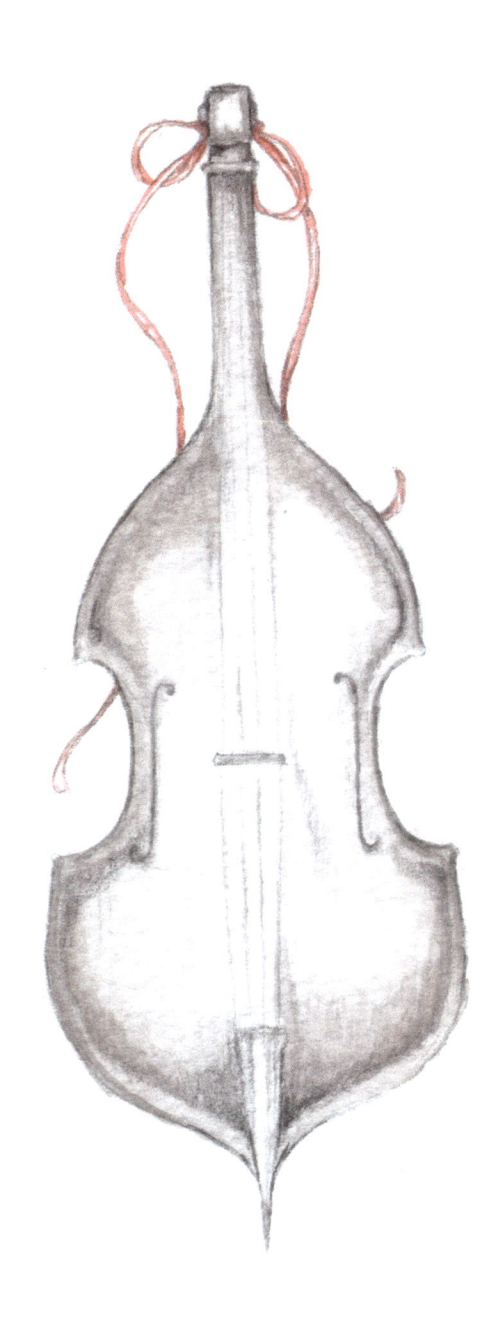

Neko loved his double bass. He loved the feel of its smooth, finely crafted wood. He loved the deep, strong sounds it made when he drew his bow across its strings. Most of all, he loved playing it in the Butterfield Symphony Orchestra. Playing music for the BSO, Neko thought, was quite possibly the best and most important thing anyone could ever do.

Night after night, Neko and the orchestra made beautiful music for all the Butterfield ladies and gentlemen. They came to hear *Pictures At An Exhibition*, which reminded Neko of the beautiful paintings he saw as he strolled through city art galleries. They closed their eyes and listened dreamily during *Swan Lake*, which filled Neko's head with images of twirling ballerinas in toe shoes and tutus. And they sat up straight and listened to Mahler's First Symphony which was dramatic and exciting and made Neko think of heroes on horseback rescuing maidens with long, flowing hair.

Neko was proud to be a member of the BSO, and he loved his job—or at least he did, until the Twiggets moved in. Neko did not love the Twiggets.

The Twiggets were orchestra mice. Mama and Papa Twigget had met years ago, when they were neighbors in the violin section. Now they were a family—Mama, Papa, and their two sets of twins, Johann and Sebastiana, and Elise and Claude.

It was the second set of twins that made Mama decide the cello they called home was just too small. Before Neko knew what was happening, the Twiggets had moved into his bass.

With all the space in Neko's bass, the children had plenty of room to play, Papa finally had a workshop to build things, and Mama had a library to store all her books about fine composers from Bach to Bartok. The Twiggets were sure they'd found the perfect home for their family. Neko was sure that a family of six—no matter how small—should not be living in his bass.

Maybe Neko could have put up with the Twiggets if they stayed out of sight. But Mama loved classical music. From the first note of a favorite symphony, she would steal out of the f-hole, climb onto the bridge, and settle in to listen. She might not have bothered Neko at all, except that she followed every move of his bow as it glided back and forth. She stared at every vibration of the strings as Neko plucked them. And when it wasn't Neko's turn to play, she nodded her head and counted with him until it was. Mama's staring made Neko nervous. Sometimes it made him so nervous that he lost his place.

Papa Twigget loved jazz. When he heard Ellington or Gershwin, he'd grab Mama's hand and pull her along as he scampered up the neck of the bass. When they reached the scroll, they giant-leaped over to the music stand where, for the rest of the concert, they *danced*. They danced fast. They danced slow. They boogied and swayed. Their dancing made Neko jumpy. Sometimes it made him so jumpy that he made mistakes.

But Mama and Papa were nothing compared to the twins. When they came out, they played hide and seek behind Neko's music and popped out unexpectedly, which made Neko jerk.

They did the limbo under the bass by his feet. They perched atop his bow and rode it like a roller coaster. Just thinking about whether or not the twins would come out was very distracting.

Sometimes Neko got so distracted that he forgot to start playing.

Ever since the Twiggets arrived, Neko was not making beautiful music for the Butterfield Symphony Orchestra. He was too nervous. He was too jumpy. He was too distracted. And Max DeNotes, the conductor, knew it.

Neko had always been afraid of Maestro DeNotes because he had one big bushy black eyebrow that made him look angry all the time. Now, Neko was even more afraid because every time he missed a note, Maestro DeNotes glared at him. And every time Maestro DeNotes glared, Neko worried that he would lose his job. Neko did not want to lose his job, because playing music in the BSO was quite possibly the best and most important thing anyone could ever do.

The Twiggets had to go.

Before the next concert, Neko was worried. Maestro DeNotes had composed a new orchestra piece that would be played for the very first time in Butterfield, and Neko had an important solo near the beginning. He could not have Mama staring at him. He could not have Papa making him jumpy. He could not have the twins distracting him. Most of all, he could not make any mistakes in Maestro DeNotes' new composition. So before the brass section players took their seats, Neko scooped up the Twiggets and stuffed them into Ben's tuba.

Max DeNotes stepped onto the podium and the orchestra began to play. The violins started, and the violas and cellos followed. Then it was Neko's turn. He raised his bow and drew it across the strings... BRAWWWWWNNNNNN. He looked down, expecting to see Mama staring at him, but she wasn't there. He kept an eye on his music, waiting for one of the twins to pop out at any moment, but none did. Neko began to relax... BRAWWWWN, DAWWWWN, BRRRAW, DAAAWW...

The music got faster, but Neko didn't lose his place. He wasn't making mistakes. Soon, the trumpets, tubas, and trombones behind him would start up, accompanying him with their deep brassy sounds. Soon after that, Neko's solo would be over. He would have played it perfectly, without any trouble from the Twiggets.

If only it had happened that way.

Neko was indeed playing beautifully when the brass section joined in. He heard the bah-bah-ba-bah of the trumpets, and waited for Ben's tuba and its rhythmic oom-pah-pahs. But when Ben blew into his tuba, nothing happened. He tried again, and nothing happened.

Finally, Ben blew as hard as he could into the big tuba, but what came out wasn't an oom-pah. It was all of the Twiggets.

From the bell of Ben's tuba, the Twiggets flew into the air. Papa landed smack on the head of the cello player in front of Neko. Mama landed on the keys of a trumpet two rows over. There she teetered, with each leg on a key, until she finally lost her balance and landed in the trumpet player's lap.

Johann and Sebastiana landed on top of Neko's bow, but lost their grip as a nervous Neko played faster and faster. They landed on Neko's strings with a horrible THRRRRRUNK and a terrible DRRRRBUNNNNN. Tiny Elise and Claude, who had been holding hands when they were launched out of the tuba, came apart and landed on each of the very startled conductor's ears. The musicians missed a beat. The audience laughed and screamed. Maestro DeNotes glared. "THAT'S IT!" he shouted at Neko. "YOU'RE FIRED!"

Neko was stunned. He tried to apologize. He wanted to explain how perfectly it all would have gone if the Twiggets had never come to the BSO, but it was hopeless. In front of the BSO and all the ladies and gentlemen of Butterfield, Neko picked up his bass and walked away from what was possibly the best and most important job anyone could ever have.

The Twiggets were right behind him.

The Twiggets felt awful about Neko losing his job. They felt even worse when they realized that without the BSO, Neko didn't want to play music. At home in his living room, Neko sat sadly in his chair while the bass gathered dust. Inside the bass, Mama tried to read but it was too quiet. Papa tried to putter in his new shop. The twins tried to amuse themselves but just got in everyone's hair until finally, Mama sent them out to play.

Outside, things were even quieter. Johann and Sebastiana tried to limbo, but without music, it wasn't much fun. Elise and Claude played hide and seek, but without music, their hearts just weren't in it. Of course riding the bow was out of the question because Neko wasn't playing. When they saw Neko's long face, the Twiggets knew they weren't the only ones who needed music. Johann shook his head and sat down hard on Neko's A string.

The string made a little "thrummm" sound. When Sebastiana heard the sound, she got an idea. She jumped onto the D string and hopped up and down... bip bip bip. Sebastiana kept hopping on the D, and Johann jumped again on the A. Thrummm, bip, bip, thrummmm, bip bip. Now Johann leaped onto the E string, then back to the A. Elise grabbed the G string with her paws and let it go.... Thrumm, bip, bip, pik, pik, thrummm, durrrrn, bip bip... They were making music!

Claude scrambled up the neck of the bass, and slid down the E string like a fireman down a fire pole, a perfect glissando. Sebastiana wriggled on her back on the G and D strings, which tickled, but made a beautiful vibrato sound. Back and forth the mice slid, hopped, and wriggled until Mama and Papa climbed out to see what was going on. When Mama saw who was making the music, she clapped her hands and laughed. She and Papa started dancing to the funky melodies. The Twiggets were having more fun than they'd had in weeks, until...

"NO, NO, NO! NOT LIKE THAT!"

Neko was up from his chair. He towered over the Twiggets, who had stopped their music and were suddenly very aware that without his bass in front of him, Neko looked very, very tall. He was about to shout again when he caught sight of his bow. Neko picked it up and gently blew off some dust. The wide-eyed Twiggets watched in silence.

"Move," Neko said. The mice jumped back. Neko pulled his bass into position and held his bow aloft. He held it there for so long that Mama Twigget began to worry. Then, he gracefully lowered it and drew it across his strings. The Twiggets smiled. Neko sighed and smiled back. He started playing from Bach's solo suites, which were always great fun.

After Bach, Neko played music by Bottesini, a great bassist who was born almost two hundred years ago. Neko finished the first piece and was beginning another when he suddenly stopped. He turned to the Twiggets, who were lined up on the table, still as statues. "Well," Neko said. "Come on." The Twiggets were puzzled, but Mama understood. She clambered up to her spot on the bridge. Papa followed, running up the neck of the bass and hopping onto the music stand. As Johann and Sebastiana started their limbo, Neko realized that he wasn't nervous, or jumpy, or distracted at all.

After that, Neko played his bass every day. He played bluegrass and jazz, classical and pop, things he had not played for a very long time and things he had never played before. Very often, he invited the Twiggets to join in and they composed their own music. It was great fun, but Neko was sad that there was nobody to hear them.

One morning, Neko took his bass to the Butterfield Music Hall. If he could play for Maestro DeNotes without making any mistakes, the conductor might give him another chance. Neko hoped so, because playing music in the BSO was quite possibly the best and most important thing anyone could ever do.

Neko was nervous when he knocked on the maestro's office door. The conductor threw it open and when he saw Neko, he glared, his two big eyes bulging from under the angry black caterpillar perched above them. Neko shook with fear. Inside the bass, the Twiggets held their breath.

"What do YOU want?" the Maestro growled, his eyebrow dancing up and down with each word. Neko was so distracted by the dancing caterpillar that he couldn't remember why he had come. When Neko didn't reply, the conductor lost patience. "Get out!" he bellowed. "I fired you!" And with that, he slammed the door.

Slowly, Neko walked out of the Butterfield Music Hall for the last time. The thought of never again playing music for the people of Butterfield made Neko so sad that he had to stop to rest. He took a seat on a street bench and sighed.

Mama knew that when Neko was sad, he didn't play music, but she knew now what to do. She called to Johann and Sebastiana, who scurried out and hopped onto Neko's strings, bum, dum, ba, da... Neko shook his head, but Mama was not about to give up. She nodded at Elise and Claude, who started plucking. She motioned to

Papa, who started dancing. Neko barely noticed any of it until Mama lay on her back on Neko's strings and shimmied for all she was worth. That made Neko smile. That made Neko pick up his bow.

Right on the street, Neko and the Twiggets played all their favorite pieces, just as if they were home in Neko's living room. People stopped to watch, and stayed to listen. Many of them liked the music so much that they threw money into Neko's bass case.

Neko and the Twiggets played until dark, until Neko's shoulders ached and his fingers were numb, until the exhausted Twiggets had barely the strength to crawl back into the bass for the trip home. Still, they couldn't wait to do it again.

Mama Twigget was full of plans. The next day, she and Papa sewed costumes for the whole family—tutus, uniforms, bright colored dresses, and tuxedos with tails. When Neko and the Twiggets played on the street, sometimes the Twiggets helped Neko play new music, and sometimes they put on dance shows that drew oohs and aahs from the crowd. Sometimes the people danced, too. Neko loved seeing so much happiness.

One day, an angry-looking man with one big bushy eyebrow stopped to watch Neko and the Twiggets. It was Maestro DeNotes. When they finished their number, he said, "Neko, would you come back to the BSO?" Neko couldn't believe his ears. He could have his job back! He could play beautiful music for all the ladies and gentlemen of Butterfield, and it would make them happy, and they would smile and applaud and ask for more…just like…they were doing…right… now!

Neko looked at the people who were cheering and clapping, and begging him to continue. They wanted to hear his music because it made them think of wonderful things like rainbows, birthday parties, and love. Before Neko could stop himself, the word was out: "No."

The maestro's eyebrow shot up in surprise, but Neko didn't care. He didn't care because playing the music he loved with his friends made him happy, and now Neko knew that was the best and most important thing anyone could ever do.

There was simply no possibly about it.

The End